D1132793

Also by Forrest Hamer

Call & Response
Terrain (chapbook)

Forrest Hamer

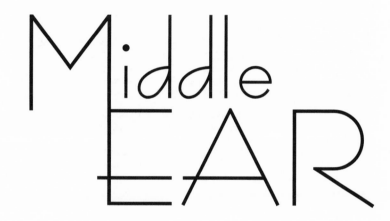

Middle
EAR

THE ROUNDHOUSE PRESS

© 2000 by Forrest Hamer

Library of Congress Cataloging-in-Publication Data
Hamer, Forrest, 1956–
      Middle ear / Forrest Hamer.
              p. cm. — (California poetry series ; v. 7)
      ISBN: 0-9666691-6-9
      1. California, Northern—Poetry. 2. Vietnamese Conflict,
1961–1975—Poetry. 3. Goldsboro (N.C.)—Poetry. I. Title. II. Series.
      PS3558.A42167 M53 2000
      811'.54—dc21   00-010862

Grateful acknowledgment is made to the following journals in which some of these poems have appeared: *Barnabe Mountain Review, Beloit Poetry Journal, Callaloo, Crab Orchard Review, Fourteen Hills, Luna, Massachusetts Review, Perihelion, Ploughshares, Poetry Flash, Shenandoah, TriQuarterly* (a publication of Northwestern University), and *ZYZZYVA*.

Several of these poems appear in the chapbook *Terrain* (with Dan Bellm and Molly Fisk, Hip Pocket Press, 1998), and in these anthologies: *Word of Mouth: An Anthology of Gay American Poetry* (Talisman House, 2000); *The Geography of Home: California's Poetry of Place* (Heyday Books, 1999); and *Times Ten: An Anthology of Northern California Poets* (Small Poetry Press, 1997). "Goldsboro Narrative" numbers 4, 7, and 28 were published together as "Goldsboro Narratives" in *Callaloo* and reprinted in *The Best American Poetry 2000*, Rita Dove and David Lehman, editors (Scribner's). "Crossroads" was reprinted on the *Poetry Daily* Web site.

This is Volume 7 of the California Poetry Series.
Cover Photo: "Songs of Faith," 1995, Como, Mississippi, by Jack Spencer.
Author Photo: Lynda Koolish
Cover and Interior Design: David Bullen Design

The California Poetry Series is published by The Roundhouse Press and distributed by Heyday Books. It is available directly from Heyday Books, or through Small Press Distribution.

Orders, inquiries, and correspondence should be addressed to:
Heyday Books
P.O. Box 9145
Berkeley, California 94709
phone: 510.549.3564   fax: 510.549.1889
e-mail: poetry@heydaybooks.com
www.heydaybooks.com

Printed in U.S.A.

10   9   8   7   6   5   4   3   2   1

Thanks to Dan Bellm, Lynne Knight, and Molly Fisk for their particular advice on the structure of this collection; as well as to David Alpaugh, Noah Blaustein, Sharon Fain, George Higgins, Jamie Irons, Alice Jones, Melody Lacina, Kathleen Lynch, and Lisa Sitkin for their helpful response to some of these poems; to Joyce Jenkins and Patricia Wakida of The Roundhouse Press; to the Squaw Valley Community of Writers and the Bread Loaf Writer's Conference. And, to our parents, whoever they are.

Contents

The Tuning

Middles we can handle but we have ends
and beginnings and what can we do about them?

WILLIAM BRONK, *The Cage of Age*

The Last Leg

        When I approach the horse hued the bluing moon,
It leans into the ground and will not be mounted.

The whinny is laughter;
I have been tricked. I can never go back.

It rains gallops the rest of that night.

Crossroads

Arrival

They say Robert Johnson couldn't play that guitar one lick
until he gave his soul away, and that his voice near itched.
Folks became amazed by the music he could make,
                                        once they listened.

Looking at birds, my friend can see the dinosaurs they were.
They scare her winging down. She can't decide the sound.

They say before he was cursed to live on his belly, give up
                        the terrible wings, Lucifer was loved.
They say that night he became a black man offering
                vision, a faithful woman, then fame,
        and each time Johnson refused. His life was more
                                        than half over, he could tell.

I believe insight doesn't happen at once.
I believe we ready ourselves that one more time and look
                differently, and change happens with small sights
        which accrete and feather. We see, we become.

When Alice and KwanLam were married, red-winged blackbirds came
from all over the grove, making the bamboo whish.

Hearing Loss

A man goes deaf because he isn't listening,

Because he lives his life as if

There is nothing here. And, of course,
There is nothing here

Saving what has been heard.

Partial

Half deaf is probably not the full truth,
for not ever hearing in one ear more likely means
only perceptible lack.

My good eyesight and sensitivity to smell
make up for some of it,
and there is always imagination. I think

that to hear twice of what I do would be
awful;
a fraction might be nice.

And maybe my eyesight and sense of smell
are the same as most everyone's.
It may well be that only my mind's ear is more

tuned, what I hear there something
from without and within; sights, too; a whole world
I have been living, alongside

the one where you and I are. I've never been sure, though.
Sometimes, it gets to be so loud
I can't hear; and, like many who appear

depressed, I withdraw.
Sometimes I miss being here.
Sometimes I miss being there.

Twelve

And my grandfather was dead for just months, and the family was unmooring, his children now the elders among us, some of them living far away.

And my father had returned to Viet Nam for another year, and this time he volunteered which made no real sense to me, the way his rules made no sense but he was leaving them behind, anyway.

And my mother was without the men she loved, and I was a boy.

And the man I looked to to take my father's place drank to the point of being a drunk, but he liked me and he liked that I liked him, even if the liking he wanted was not the liking I felt.

And I grew what looked like a foot of inches, suddenly, my body reaching at its final height.

And Martin Luther King was murdered, and the town instantly set a curfew, and everyone in the North End stayed inside, all fury and despairing eager to find the way out.

And the Emancipation Proclamation was what people kept talking about, as if words by themselves could describe that freedom.

And Master Woodard told him he could stay on the plantation and become one of their farming assistants.

And from the playground the sixth-graders had all to ourselves, we watched the marchers carrying tall signs, the woman with the deep voice looking straight at me and saying, We're causing this trouble for *you.*

And he left his master, glad, wondering would he want to remember, and who ever would remember him in the far from now.

And I lost interest in any history but becoming 13.

And there was a freedom I could imagine.

And my best friend was my cousin Larry, who was my age and kept secrets.

And the boys just older formed a group we could belong to if we passed one at a time through their gauntlet.

And the 14 children who would be born and who would die waited for him to leave sharecropping, meet Jemima Thompson and become the man who is their father.

And he would tell himself as Benjamin Barnes, born in 18 and 53, who had been called already to be a preacher.

And he tended beans, cotton, corn, and peanuts.

And for the first time I cropped tobacco, cropped for four days, the misery of which I would not tell excepting my cousin and my brother and my aunt.

And his friend from the plantation was Willie; they laughed with each other about things, and he promised he would name a son the name of his friend.

And he loved the sound of his freedom, and he sang it often.

And in my bed I felt myself burning between the pajamas and my stomach, and it was a new happiness.

And I began not liking church music, wanting instead to dance on Sundays, especially the Boogaloo.

And I wanted my father's permission by mail to get a Quo Vadis haircut, promising now I would take care of my hair.

And he began thinking someday he could marry.

And my cousin and I debated the meanings of soul, and wondered when our people would become free.

And those of us afraid of snakes were sent each to capture one and to care for it, and those of us afraid of heights were sent to the roof of the North End School to stand at the ledge and to look.

And I asked to keep my Papa Willie's pocket watch, the one with the second hand bent and the crystal chipped.

And he began making long walks, farther away and back.

And he figured the world laid before him good, anyway, despite the stark hatreds.

And he thought all the days and nights of that year only of freedom.

Encounter

You tell yourself what it's like; that, exactly,
Not evil, not the devil

you can tell. And when you hear what
Not a man, his dark birds

it's like from someone else, a stranger you are
Not night, but keener wish

walking with because there is this chance,
Not the soul changing form

you sense what you've known all along.
But the bargain

Await

yes, I foreknew this one come along a bleak night
near these rivers talking himself almost a song—

And if I give myself for mere imagination,
And if I give myself for this imagination,
Then what else could I do.

Argument Against

As if a black man middling age finally
subject of the poem   As if all poems need

to be written   As if the middle

of a life is one moment of mind
As if crossing the river Jordan

As if the body supposes but the poem reaches (toward), and
as if all things (the poem too a thing) must exist

As if the man could write about anything

else   As if this man would live   As if to say *the self,*
still (body and poem now one)

As if a lover, a journey
And, — *there*

a man writes his dark body and some of its assumptions,
this the text of his preaching

As if the body fails because the man fails

crossing over, river receded   As if there, *but then*

Middle Ear

Say that moment crossing over isn't heard
Say the hammer-anvil-stirrup don't unfurl
Say the balance was upset

Say this balance was upset
Say the outside world doesn't ring

Say the mind's ear listening to an odd man singing
Say the moment crossing over starting somewhere out and in
Say the balance was upset

Say this balance was upset, and the singing falls faint
Say you turn yourself away from crowds of sound

Say the awed man singing sings to you

Say you don't know him. You don't.

And the balance is upset

Say the inside singing and the outside ringing and
    the moment crossing over breathing in
Say the whisper of the man sieves through
Say the moment crossing over is a stranger wisp

And the balance is upset
And the balance is upset

Say the moment crossing over rights the left
Say the moment crossing over is the ringing ear writing
Say the moment crossing over ends hear

Origins

Thinking he was asking about race, I told him I was black;
and, thinking he was asking where I come from, I told him
I was from the South and from here in California and, really,
I am from the people I love who love me; and, thinking
he was asking about my sexual orientation, I told him, yes,
I am sexually oriented, especially with some men; then,
thinking he was asking about my religion, I told him I had none
to speak of except for my awe of the spirit; and, hearing
him ask specifically where I was coming from, I told him then
I come from wherever it is strangers tell their lives
in ways far less specific than speaking to each other dreams,
which is how, if I had been thinking, I should have told him
about myself.

Sign

Consider the bird.
Consider the dreamer who witnesses a bird flinging
                into a church, the windows yawned open.
Consider whose death will follow.

Consider the flinging.

Consider the time between sign and dying, time nothing
                to do with the bird or the witness or the waiting.
Consider their congregation.
Consider the sermon near middle when the bird comes.

Consider the bound ceiling, and the jerking bird zig-zagging about.

Consider that the death would be sudden.
Consider the old.
The funeral-tired, the hymn-weary, arm-weak.

Considering flinging.

Consider, congregation.
The hovering flutters stuck.
A promise.

Each, every proof.

Crossroads

Crossed over the river and the river went dry
Crossed over the river, the river went dry
Saw myself drowning and I couldn't see why

Come up for air and the day said noon
Come up for air, said the air read noon
Day said, Son, you better mind something soon

Sink back down, felt my spirits leave high
Sink back down, I felt my spirits lift high
Didn't know if I was gonna die

A man give his hand and he pulled me to the shore
Man give his hand, pulled me over to the shore
Told me if I come I wouldn't drown no more

Me and the man walked and talked all day and night
Me and the man, we walked, we talked all day and night
We started wrestling til the very lip of light

I put my mind on evil sitting in my soul
Put my mind on evil just a-sitting on my soul
Struggling with the devil make a soul old

I looked at my face and my life seem small
Looked hard at my face and this life it look so small
All of a sudden didn't bother me at all

Returned to the river and I stood at the shore
Went back to the river and I stood right at the shore
Decided to myself needn't fight no more

13 Suppositions about the Ubiquitous

Suppose your life were a body.
Suppose in the middle of the body you began to die.

Suppose your life lost all its hungers, and in the minute you were
full and not desiring, you noticed a voice from the inner ear
singing names.
Suppose you listened to yourself.

Suppose you suddenly budded wings, and you were lifted above earth
and you looked down to see your kin looking for you.
Suppose the body is a new lesson.

Supposing middle.

Suppose the curiosity of a child imagining through clothes is first
evidence of dying.
Suppose your body wants another's, but will only come into it for what is
a long minute each time.

Suppose you suddenly bud wings, and you lift yourself over earth
and look back to see your kin looking for you, but you are not yourself.
Suppose you are listening.

Suppose in the middle of your body you begin to die.
Suppose the body the beginning.

The Different Strokes Bar, San Francisco

Maybe I knew it wouldn't last long, that the joys of us
could vanish like ghosts having lost interest.
Maybe I knew there would be more
than the early twenties of this life, the body quicking.
Maybe I could see men dancing themselves invisible,
one by handsome one, that year before they began to go.
So when I told my friend to stop dancing,
stop with me in the middle of the floor and remember this,
how wondrous already it was, I must have known
how easy it is to forget, how easy it is not to notice,
the dancing going on all about
your new and hungry body, you taken away with it.

Bargain

Goldsboro Narrative #4:
My father's Viet Nam tour near over

The young dead soldier was younger
than they thought: the 14-year-old passed
himself as seventeen, forged
a father's signature. In the Army no more
than months, he was killed early
the week before a cease-fire.
The boy was someone-I-somewhat-knew's
older brother and someone-my-mother-
had-taught's son, and, lying
in the standard Army casket, an American
flag draped over the unopened half,
the boy didn't look like anyone
anybody would know—a big kid his dark skin
peached pale, lips pouted. I was sure
I didn't recognize him.

      When kids older than us
closed down one campus after another,
I thought they'd close all colleges down,
and there would be no place for me
when it was my time. It didn't seem fair.

      Capt. Howell's wife answered
the door one day, and two men
in military dress asked to come in.
She had no choice, I suppose,
but once they came into her living room,
she no longer had a husband, and
the three boys and the girl no longer
had their father. *So this is how
it happens,* I thought: two men come
to your house in the middle of the day,

ringing a bell or rapping on the door.
And, afterwards, there's nothing left
to look forward to.

Usher

The night the Walker Bible College picketed
the Paramount, we were showing the orgy movie
where everybody gorged on chocolate,
one of them a tall guy who kept dipping
his angling penis into what looked to me
like semi-sweet. Jack Blount bet it was
bittersweet, a flavor he'd never got to liking.

Ten minutes in, during the first sex scene,
Jack and I left to set out marquee letters
for the Sunday children's matinee. By the time
we put up the ladder, there were more picketers
than patrons, and even the actors on screen
got distracted by the noise: some man began
to preach and then he kind of danced,

and everybody followed with those chants
Jack said he would have liked hadn't it been
for that ladder-rocking the dancing made.
Ecstatic, somebody brought out the chocolate,
bringing the actors back to their business.
A few minutes before credits, we went to open
the doors at the back, and Jack told me

he thought he'd seen that dancing man
four or five times at the late shows, thought
this was that guy who always left just
as we opened the lobby doors, before
the movie really ended, missing what can happen,
Jack said, when the man urgent and dripping
with chocolate asks if anyone else wants a lick.

Caught

When Mitch's mother caught us fondling each other,
She was most assuredly angry, saying
We were doing wrong, that if we didn't stop
We'd end up funny and what kind of life would that be.

We'd been getting careless. She certainly scared us.
I feared she'd tell my family what she'd seen,
But I was relieved to know Mitch and I were not yet funny
Which is probably why we became even more

Daring with each other, no longer courting
Uncertainty, touching each other
Wherever we wanted, then when, one body familiar
As the other. We still had lots of time.

Goldsboro Narrative #28

When folks caught on to what was happening
between Rev. Johnson and Sister Edna,
the grown-ups went back to speaking
in front of children as if we couldn't spell.
It was easy to figure out, though:
Rev. Johnson's wife didn't get happy; and,
after service, she wouldn't shake hands
with Sister Edna or any of her kin.
And Sister Edna's husband, Mr. Sam,
who never came to church, began waiting
in the parking lot to drive his wife home.

Now the age Rev. Johnson was then, I doubt
he was concerned with being forgiven.
But when I was 12 and kept on falling
from available grace, I began dismissing him
and mostly all of what he said he meant.
I went witnessing instead to Mr. Sam,
his truck idling outside the paned windows,
him dressed in overalls and a new straw hat.

Witness

It was enough to ruin a friendship—
breaking the promise not to tell, not even to talk
about it, not to tell his girlfriend

he had skipped his art class and I my chemistry lab
to be in a police line up, both of us
tall and black and medium-complected, both of us

willing to do someone else a favor
and go down to the main New Haven Police Station
so there would finally be enough of us,

some of us Yalies and some of us townies, none of us
saying very much as we entered the station
crowded with black men and brown men, all of us

waiting to go in the rooms and stand in a line.
When it was time, we each got a number
to hold and it was clear this was no ordinary favor

no interesting academic study no joke no
experience to talk about at parties or on vacation
at home not even some small way of helping

to end the rapes that had been happening on campus
to white women who sat with us in class or
in dining halls or sometimes lived across the hall.

One by one, we stepped out of line, turned
left, turned back front, stepped back. One by one.
And the one of us brought in in chains

seemed dull and out of step with us. And, after,
the Yalies got in a van, rode silently back.
My friend who had not looked at me asked me not to tell

his girlfriend where we'd been. I told him I would not.
I forgot. I couldn't say why, but I forgot
not to tell her. But when he came to me angry to talk,

I remembered, and I was ashamed and sorry.
It was enough to ruin a friendship. Ten months before,
our friendship new and already deep, we honored

our first Thanksgiving away from the families we'd come from,
homes we missed much more than we'd even expected.
After dinner, a white couple came over to tell us they'd been watching

and they wanted us to know how nice we seemed
to be, the difference we were from the other blacks they knew,
how kind to each other we seemed.

For a moment, my friend and I looked away from each other
and into the faces of those who stood smiling.
One of us asked where they'd come from, the other how soon

they'd be gone. We went back to the meal, talking but not
talking about the white couple from Detroit.
Then something mute came and sat at our table, waiting.

Moving On

1.

When my father finally spoke to me
about war, he didn't mention Viet Nam
but a bone-chill Korea, cleaved into before
I was born. And he told me a white man
saved his life there, the white man

his friend, another Southerner
away from home for the first time.
Billy McGee saw the land mine
my father almost tripped, and he moved him
out of the way. When McGee moved on,

2.

stateside, my father said he missed him
openly and for days, until another
white soldier, also a Southerner,
told my father what the other whites knew,
that McGee belonged to the Klan

back in South Carolina, and he'd boasted
he was even one of their leaders.
My father's sadness ended quick, he said,
and he never wrote the letters he had
promised, never heard again from McGee.

3.

My father hasn't told me I could tell this.
He didn't say I could show the naive love
he can have for men, how ashamed a man
who is also a black man can be when
a white man saves his life. But when he says

he doesn't care whatever happened
to Billy McGee, he hasn't told me
not to wonder whether people do move
each other in the end, or if saving
someone's story is the same as saving life.

4.

During my father's second Viet Nam tour,
something between us changed—he came back startled
and quiet. And I began demanding
he let me wear my hair long and in braids.
We seemed to find no more to say, so

I plotted to leave my father's house.
Once every few months, after some fight,
I asked him what had happened over there.
There was nothing to tell me, he said:
he came home, a lot of others didn't.

5.

Leaving a father's house is never as easy
as moving away. For a long time, sometimes
always, one of them, the father, the child,
wishes away ever having loved the other,
and the other resents being loved this way.

When I became grown, and my father began ending
the rest of his life, he finally told me
about war and the man there who saved him.
My father told me that was the blessing
I'd wanted. He asked me to give him mine.

Goldsboro Narrative #33

These usually quiet men, these dignified
and dressed well men
seemed bowed by the week between Sundays,
by too many hours at work, or by no work,
or not enough work.

Even the Spirit seemed partial to their wives
and mothers,
And each third Sunday in June
when the Men's Chorus sang,
we half expected them to wail out at us,

boys distracted by vague travels we would make
once we left
our mothers who kept bringing us here,
once we could run roads
conjured from the ink

of funeral-home fans with pictures of a white Jesus,
laying out
long streets to have fights on,
where we could own things
and grow big, have what we needed.

But Mr. Joe's voice trembled, too deep and too loud
to fit,
and it reminded us he had gone away
but come back.
Because the men liked him, they didn't mind

how much his voice startled their babies,
distracted the wives.
They wanted him singing with them.
Usually he sang two solos,
the bass part only.

Children dared themselves to hum along
in alto or in tenor.
And each year, after Mr. Joe finished, mothers
looked back into the eyes
of all of the boys in the congregation,

expecting we had learned something.

Goldsboro Narrative #7

Time was a boy, specially a black boy,
need to be whipped by his kin, teach him
not to act up, get hisself killt.
Folks did this cause they loved they boys.
The man laughs. And boys would do what all
they could to get out of them whippings,
play like they was getting tore up,
some play like they was going to die.
My grandmama the first one that whipped me,
and she made me get my own switches.
If I come back to her with a switch too small,
she make me go right back and get a big one.
And she whipped me for that, too. He laughs.
I loved that woman, though. Sho did.

Annual Visit of the Quiet, Unmarried Son

After my mother kissed my sleeping father,
she kissed me and thanked God for letting me see
the New Year, for many had not been so blessed.

She talked about her friend Mr. James,
months before murdered in a night of profound disappointments,
the wounds in couples all over

his body (even under his feet),
the handsome young lover who killed him when wronged,
the old mother left grieving,

the many at his wake, the way he looked then
—like a boy just calming after a nightmare,
they say: my mother had stayed away,

that the man who found the shreds of the body
has not been the same, that no one nearby heard
a sound. I wanted to scream at her to stop

and I wanted her to tell me everything she'd heard,
my mother reckoning on into morning
with something hurt between us, still unmentioned.

Charlene–N–Booker 4Ever

And the old men, supervising grown grandsons, nephews,
any man a boy given this chance of making
a new sidewalk outside the apartment building where
some of them live, three old men and their wives,
the aging unmarrying children, and the child
who is a cousin, whose mother has sent her here
because she doesn't know what to do with her,
she's out of control, she wants to be a gangsta, and
the old folks talk to her as if she minds them
and already has that respect for their years her mother
finally grew into. The girl who does not look
like them eats and eats and sleeps late, sneaks away
when they are busy, and tonight will write herself
all over the sidewalk while it is still wet but
the old have gone inside, and the grown gone home,
and her mother who is somewhere overseas thinks of
writing her that long long letter, but decides not to.

Exorcism

Who spoke himself through her took away her voice.

And since she had not been herself,
the church mothers convened to cast him out of her.

Reverend Telitha and Reverend Fannie,
Cousin Athenia and Cousin Lila and Aunt Maggie
and one or two more I don't remember—

Come back. Come on back.

—made circle around her, summoning water.
They chanted.
Laid hands on Berniece's head.

And then the mothers abandoned themselves.

Their bodies still holding each other called out.
Not now. Pray don't leave me now.

Who was banished into his sea of want.

Reverend Telitha revenant.
She thanked Jesus. Berniece Lane whisting
Jesus, Jesus

Grace

This air is flooded with her. I am a boy again,
and my mother and I lie on wet grass, laughing. She startles,
turns to marigolds at my side, saying *beautiful,*
and I can see the red there is in them.

When she would fall into her thoughts, we'd look for what
distracted her from us.

My mother's gone again as suddenly as ever
and, seven months after the funeral,
I go dancing.
I am becoming grateful. Breathing, thinking, *marigolds.*

Edge

My mother told my sister that dying had hurt, but only a little; and then
She was somewhere other than she had been.

Probably, there are endless states of mind, and we live so much in them
Transitions seem something like suffering, which is also a state of mind.

I remember a Dillard High School homecoming parade down Elm Street.
The band showed off, and pretty girls draped over cars and floats.
A new tune by the Supremes blew through air, and, as far as
I was concerned, this day was beginning and end of the world.

I see that just across Elm Street, a cemetery stayed
Behind the dull brick wall. And because
Only white people were buried there, and perhaps because black people
Could not be, the cemetery was not there,
The bodies beneath all those gravestones not there.

In the Middle

I could be wrong, but I think my life is half over.
I think this because of a dream I had a few years ago about a house.
It was my new home. Mostly. It was unfinished.

The house was a circle resting above a story and overlooking trees.
Each room was different and each room had two doorways but no doors,
so coming in and leaving was very easy.
The dream conceived in my conception, cells of me
beginning their own end.
Showing me halfway through my house. The unfinished home.

In a dream I had one year—more a dream about something else
than being 39—I recognized a mere idea
was stopping me from crossing a threshold.
It was like news. It changed me in a small way.

I have an idea about aging.
It is not the same as aging; the body will do as it has been doing.
But there is now less time before death
than there is from being conceived.
It startles me I think about dying
through cliches and dreams I don't author.

In the dream about the unfinished home the rooms are warm
and quite light.

When the floorboards are done, when white paint covers the plaster,
I would bring in the furniture.
I may not need doors.

The truth is I am waiting for the next dreams.
The last one has to be perfect.

In the movie *Six Degrees of Separation,* Will Smith pretends to be a man pretending to be the son of Sidney Poitier. Twice, when the character kisses other men, Will Smith avoids actually kissing the other actor, leaving that pretense to us.

Someone I know thinks I look like Sidney Poitier. I tell him, you should see my father and his brothers. I say, when I was young and Poitier came on the screen, I thought for a moment my father had come back.

In the movie *Smoke Signals,* one of the characters cuts his hair when he learns why his father left him years ago. And though the story of cut hair foretells something of what happens to the son, anyone can tell, can't you?, the actor is wearing a wig.

Before my father lost interest in the movies, he would watch the same movie over and over, not realizing he had seen it already. I would say to him, don't you remember? And he would shush me, because I was distracting him.

The Tuning

Source

The first sound is hers, harmonic heart-beat

Which for a time is all there is in music; later,
What there is exists against her and her tongue,
The songs she sings to sleep you or to feed,

You there with your terrors and your silence.

Summon

Tell of it, before

Before I came into the body that is this
Before all of my life placed from its center

Before I was called to listening
Before I answered saying, I AM HERE AND UNFORMED

Before the world waits brilliant as body of the lover
Well—

Before long gone rains return to us breathing
Before these winds

Before I am known with another
Before I begin to forget

Then, Amen.

Yea, before all of this which is absence—

Tone-deaf

Then, turning a heavy ear there, we hear nearly

Everything, too too much,

So it seems like nothing at all, not attuning

Imagination, not a chance, not one

Soul faithful and still, on key.

Instrument

Each note has its noise—approximations, clack
Each finger keens against slack wire.

And each noise notes this memory:

Loneliest in things:

                wrested triumph,   Next and necessary loss.

The Tuning

Or say the instrument was a body, a dark one,

his own, this body becoming improbable,

bargained away into almost nothing, breathing

alone and finally beginning

to die all over again, skin liquid and fine.

Emerging, Specific

Almost. He almost had her; but,
filled with his ecstasy of almost   *(all and most)*
having her again, Orpheus looked

back.
Not content to animate the dead
world, not content with knowing,   *(and with knowing he had done nothing*
                                                        at first, had done nothing
                                                        that first time—)

he looked again and lost her.
Once more and (now) for ever.
Just his luck:

In a song he sings about rain, the gods weep for their children
but only when it is time to weep over foolishness.
After this season passes, the gods return to encouraging desire.

              : she has forgotten him.

              : when she has come above the underearth, he sees each time
                she is not the one he has gone looking for.
                The truth is : : there is no one he has gone looking for.

What, then, is his sight?   *One moved to him by raining?*
                                                  She who bore him deeply?
                                                  He who would lie with him?

(And his loss?)

                                                  He thinks. He supposes. He assumes.

The water washed them back up. After the hurricanes, a Princeville man dreamed he saw his parents once more alive, sitting in the back of his church, holding hands. They told him to be strong once more. And once more, when he buried them, he hoped this would be the last time he had to put them back into the earth.

Poets write too much about death, or at least **someone I know** thinks so. I say to him, most of the people I grew up knowing are dead, and their cemetery is becoming my neighborhood, and he says to me, but what about the body?

When we buried my mother, we had her placed in the wrong grave. The next day we learned we'd put her where my aunt will someday be, so we had to arrange to have her new vault dug up and moved. We felt awful, nervous she was furious with us, and began only then to know we had other feelings about her leaving so abruptly.

During the worst thunderstorms, we'd stretch across the width of my aunt's bed and our grandparents curled beside us, saying we should respect storms, breathe in the liquid air, go to sleep.

Shaping the Dark

The mind reposes, and a girl nearing four once more can't sleep
through the night.

And her parents tell her this time she cannot come back
to them, she must return to her room.

She hates them for this.
All kinds of monsters begin to scare her.

And the next night the girl begs to be saved from monsters,
but her parents say no, and the girl cries and cries

and her parents feel cursed.
The monsters grow in their numbers, one becoming so scary

she is funny; and the girl, stunned by the silence
of evening, walks for hours through the halls of her home.

She looks in nightlights and in streetlights
and in moonlight for shapes that will one day dress the dead.

And when the shapes move, they quiver bright with sound.
This is a comfort to her. This is her pleasure in them.

With them, she begins singing.

Testimony

Now, and then, I regret the years I live without

sound, not writing towards it,
the years not only before,when I am

a child, but later, when I then know
writing and leave it anyway, because

I am afraid, because I have nothing

yet to say. It's like the way
my mother speaks of her years without God, the service

and its blessings ever lost. But God, ever
patient, wondering when she comes to find herself

what she'll have to say.

Unnamed

Sometimes I say exactly what I mean.

Usually, I don't.

It isn't that I'm timid or a liar or prone to deceiving myself.

It's how unwise speaking often is,

Words meaning what they do.

Taking Leave

Turning to go, I also know
I can hear now.

Before I knew this, I would say
I couldn't,

And what a sorrow that seemed.

The *California Poetry Series* was created to showcase and document the literary energy of the Golden State, and to celebrate the wide range of aesthetics, cultures, and geography in California poetry. The books feature work by poets with strong ties to California. Four volumes will be released annually. The series is a collaboration: Malcolm Margolin, Heyday Books, is publisher. Joyce Jenkins, *Poetry Flash,* is series editor.

An advisory board of prominent poets and cultural leaders has been assembled to encourage and support California poetry through this book series. These include Alfred Arteaga, Chana Bloch, Christopher Buckley, Marilyn Chin, Karen Clark, Wanda Coleman, Gillian Conoley, Peter Coyote, Jim Dodge, Lawrence Ferlinghetti, Jack Foley, Jewelle Gomez, Robert Hass, Jane Hirshfield, Fanny Howe, Lawson Inada, Jaime Jacinto, Diem Jones, Stephen Kessler, William Kistler, Carolyn Kizer, Steve Kowit, Dorianne Laux, Philip Levine, Genny Lim, Suzanne Lummis, Lewis MacAdams, David Mas Masumoto, David Meltzer, Deena Metzger, Carol Muske-Dukes, Jim Paul, Kay Ryan, Richard Silberg, Gary Snyder, Dr. Kevin Starr, David St. John, Sedge Thomson, Alan Williamson, and Gary Young.

California Poetry Series books are available at bookstores nationwide or by subscription ($40.00/year). For more information:

California Poetry Series
c/o The Roundhouse Press
P.O. Box 9145
Berkeley, CA 94709
phone: 510-549-3564 fax: 510-549-1889
e-mail: poetry@heydaybooks.com